MACMILLAN READERS
STARTER LEVEL

PHILIP PROWSE

L. A. Detective

My name is Lenny Samuel.
My friends call me Len.
I'm a detective. I work
in Los Angeles. I'm an
L.A. detective.

Everybody in Los Angeles is busy.
But Len isn't busy. He's sitting
in his office. He's waiting. He has
no work today. Nothing is happening.

Then a man comes into the office. Len doesn't know him. The man is short and dark. He's about forty years old. He's wearing a suit.

The man is holding a gun. The gun is pointing at Len.

I'm Frank. Come with me. Mr Blane wants to speak to you.

I won't go with you, Frank. I don't like Mr Blane. I don't want to speak to him.

Frank is a tough man. He laughs.
He hits Len on the head. He hits
Len hard. Len's eyes close. Len
falls down. He falls onto the
floor of the office.

4

Len wakes up. He opens his eyes.
He's sitting in a big chair.
The room is very warm. There are
lots of plants in the room.

Where am I?

Hello, Mr Samuel.
Welcome to my house.

An old man is talking and smiling.
He's Mr Blane. He's a very rich man.
He's also a very bad man.

Mr Blane gives Len a photo. He says,
'I want Carmen back. Go to the bus station
at two o'clock on Tuesday. Frank has
the $100 000. He's going with you.
Give the money to The Young Ones.
Bring Carmen home. I'll pay you $1000.'

Len says, 'I don't like you, Blane.
I don't want your money. But
Carmen is in trouble. She needs help.
I'll help her.'

It's 2 pm on Tuesday. Frank and Len are at the bus station. Frank has $100 000 in a bag.

SAN FRANCISCO

Large buses are going in and out of the bus station. There are lots of people. But Len can't see Carmen.

Frank opens the bag. The young man sees the money. The young man lets go of Carmen's arm.

Len holds Carmen's arm. Frank gives the bag of money to the young man.

10

Suddenly, Carmen bites Len's hand.
Len lets go of Carmen's arm.

The young man hits Frank.
Frank falls down.

Carmen and the young man jump onto the bus. The door of the bus closes. The bus drives off. It's going to San Francisco.

SAN FRANCISCO

Len can't get on the bus. He decides to get his car. Len decides to drive to San Francisco.

12

It's Thursday. Len is in San Francisco. San Francisco is a big city. Len can't find Carmen.

Suddenly, Len sees a sign on a building.

The sign says: The Young Ones. The building is a school for poor children. Carmen is playing with the children.

Len stops his car. He goes to speak to Carmen.

14

It's Friday. Len is in Los Angeles.
He's at the police station. Frank and
Blane are at the police station too.

These papers show that
you're a criminal, Blane.

I'm tired. I have no money.
But I have an exciting job.
And I like to help people.
That's why I'm an L.A. detective.